MW01267755

One young man reveals., with honesty and humor, his experiences during WW II from basic training though the fight as an aviation radio-radarman and gunner.

I REMEMBER

World War II

by

Lucius Agee

PREFACE

The purpose of this writing is to provide my descendants and other interested readers with a record of my personal experiences and insights into World War II. I was not a hero, but I was a servant of our country. I did no more or no less than the others in my squadron. This is what happened to one person and is being published at the insistence of readers who believe others should know how the war looked and felt to a young man during life threatening, yet, friend bonding conditions. Our jobs, tasks of the mere soldiers, had a world impact, but each experience was unique, effected by the situation and the personality of each of us.

The time of this writing: 1996

Further Explanation

When I visited Aunt Lucy and Uncle Lucius after they had moved to an assisted living home, I was surprised to discover that that he was much more than a successful, creative business man. He is an author and an artist, with an acute memory. He gave me a copy of a printed book he had authored and typed himself on a typewriter.

His story telling ability and the emotions he brought to this reader gave an illusion of sitting with him and hearing it firsthand. The memories of one soldier should be published to inform other generations, to jog the memories of the few remaining veterans of World War II, and to give motivation to other veterans who have a story. His story is not a relentless tear jerker, but we know the tears are leaking when he leaves home and in various war circumstances. The mixture of laughter he managed amid the destruction and disruption gives our heart a lift and our respect for the ordinary soldier rises to new heights.

Because of his natural voice, the story, with very little editing, remains as he personally typed it. He speaks his story. Other fascinating stories not contained in this publication reveal the effort of his widowed mother, his determination to get an education, his love for his wife and family and the efforts of a Tennessee youngster taking advantage of the American opportunity to build a successful business.

Assistant publisher: Maxie Fortner

Chapter 1 In *the beginning*

I was drafted into the armed forces August 12, 1943. I took my physical and was sworn in at Chattanooga, Tennessee. I was put in charge of all the recruits during our travel to the "Great Lakes Naval Training Center" because I had R.O.T.C. in high school. I didn't know much. The only travel I had done was from Smith County, Tennessee, to Nashville, Tennessee. We went by train and had to transfer in Chicago at a large busy station. With the help of the other boys, green like me, we made our connection.

In boot camp, we were restricted to base and put through a rigorous training and discipline course.

One day we were on the grinder marching and I was called out to lead the group. The grinder was a large field with small gravel. As we marched we could hear the gravel grinding under all our feet is why it was called the *grinder*. There were about fifty in our group and there were several groups on the field. I was surprised when they called me out to lead our group but realized it was because I had taken R.O. T.C. in high school.

So, I started out, "Forward March! To the rear March! To the left March! By the left flank March!" and so on. After a few minutes of this I began to give commands faster with a lot of "Left flank, Right flank" mixed in. Suddenly, I realized we were headed in to a barracks building and I could not get my tongue and mind to say, "To the rear, March!". Instead I said, "STOP!" Of course. everybody laughed and the guy in charge said, "Ok, Mac! Get back in line." So that was the end of that.

★ ★ ★

One night I had to stand fire watch. This consisted of making rounds of several barracks and punching a recording device at key locations. In one of the barracks on second floor, there were several rows of two level beds. The room was dark except for red lights here and there. I could hear grunts and noises coming from one end of the building. I walked slowly until I came up on the source, and then I snapped on my bright flash light. There lay a boy on his back with his arms and legs spread out. They were tied to the bed springs with clothes stops. (I. E. cords about like shoe strings used to tie up rolled up clothes) Someone had tied him up in his sleep as a joke and he was trying to get loose without anyone knowing it. I hollered, "What is going on here?" With this someone turned on the lights and just about everybody got up to see what was going on. Everybody was laughing except the boy tied up. After a few minutes, he was untied, and I turned out the lights as I left.

Naval Aviation
has a place for You...
Pilots Machinist's Mates
Radiomen Metalsmiths
Ordnancemen

apply today

Chapter 2 *Boot Camp*

At boot camp, we took a lot of tests. As a result, I qualified to go to several service schools. I chose Aviation Radioman School.

After boot camp I was ordered to U. S. Naval Air Station, Millington, Tennessee, to attend a six-month school for aviation radiomen.

The school was strict and regimental. The day started out early in the morning before daylight with a shrill whistle followed by, "Hit the deck!" In five minutes, we had to be in front of the barracks for calisthenics. We had to march to the chow hall and to and from all our classes. There were loud speakers all along the sidewalks which played marching music.

In a few weeks, we were allowed to go to town on Saturday, provided we passed inspection on Saturday morning. This was a very tough inspection with officers who delighted in making it tough. The floor had to be steel wool rubbed and waxed to a high polish, all lockers and beds in perfect order, and all bathroom fixtures shining even on the underside. The inspector wore white gloves. He would rub his fore finger over the top of the door trim, the back of the commode, the top of a locker or anywhere he chose. If he had a discolored glove when he finished, we would be restricted to base. This required a lot of work! We did not have anyone in charge, so we had to organize and divide up the work. If someone was lazy or tried to goof off, he was told off by everyone else. If we failed inspection, the people responsible were given a hard time for the rest of the week.

One of the things we had to do was learn to take and send Morris Code by hand at twenty-one words per minute. At this speed, if I had to think for split second what a letter was, I would miss the next letter. The messages being sent were coded letters, so you could not recognize words. I had trouble and was called in to the review board. I was given two weeks to get my code up to speed. Radiomen who flunked out were sent to New Orleans to be radiomen aboard LST's. (Landing ship tank) Obviously, I did not want to flunk. After one more week I still could not get the speed. I had just about given up in my second week when, *all at once*, I was getting it all down.

One day they got us out of the barracks and put us in a long single file line and started marching us down a long sidewalk. We looked off to our left about a hundred yards and there was another long line of soldiers marching just like us. When we got to a certain spot both line of people came side by side and marched together into a large empty building without inside walls. As we marched, one line went to one side and the other line went to the opposite side. We now knew what was happening because, in the middle of the room were a lot of pads laying on the floor. It was apparent that a wrestling match was about to begin, and the contestants were *us*. The first boys in each line had to wrestle and so on down the line with no changing places for body type.

When my time came, I had to wrestle a man about fifty pounds heavier than I was. The first thing, he threw me to the mat and I landed on my stomach. He then dived, trying to land on top of me, but saw what he going to do and I slid back real fast. He landed on his stomach right in front of me. I moved up on top of him with my right arm around his head and my left arm around his left leg. With this hold he couldn't get up, but I couldn't pin him either. Finally, he got into a position with his shoulder half way on the mat. The referee was right there, and he counted three pats on the mat. I will have to say they were pretty fast pats, but I was declared the winner. My side let out a roar of approval. Everybody had their own story that night

.☆ ☆ ☆

.

On the base was a row of old airplanes that wouldn't fly but they had good radios in them. They used them to train *us*. We would man our planes, set up our transmitters, report in to the tower, and send messages back and forth. Sometimes the instructors would do something to the equipment, so it would not work. We had to figure out what was wrong and fix it. All messages were sent by Morris code. WAVES (Women Accepted for Volunteer Emergency Service) were instructors in the tower. Some of them were not very good because they could not maintain a steady rhythm.

We had a full page of "Q" signals used for short cutting messages. For example, "QSA" means "What is my bearing in relation to you?" There was one unofficial "Q" signal that everybody knew but it wasn't written down. It was "QQQ", which means "Get the bird shit off your antenna and stop sending with your foot!" Well, one day, one of the guys sent this back to the tower. Boy, did he make a mistake! All messages were copied down and reviewed by high ranking officers who made an example of him. He was out the gate with all his gear on his shoulder by 8:00 the next morning on his way to New Orleans and an "LST".

When we were near the end of radio school training, a high-ranking officer came to check out the school. When inspection came everybody of out in formation in our dress uniform. Finally, I could see them coming way down the line. There was the high-ranking officer, the captain of the base, the executive officer, and the executive officer and orderlies for all of them. When they got to about where I was, they stopped. The high-ranking officer eyed all of us and motioned for me to come forward. I didn't know what for, but I obeyed when he said, "Follow us."

Here we went, back down the line with me tagging along, I still didn't know what was up. Finally, we turned and went into one of our classroom buildings. The high-ranking officer then went over to a big radio transmitter that was used in our engine long range aircraft. He told me, "Take this frequency down. I want to set it up on this transmitter. I am going to time you."

As he watched his watch, he said, "Get ready. Go!" As luck would have it, I knew just what to do and I didn't make any false moves. As soon as I was done, I stepped back with my right hand on the key and my left hand pointing to the amp meter showing a signal was going out. I could see a broad grin on the captain's face standing behind the Officer. I was the test case for the entire school. We passed!

After graduating, we were promoted to third class petty officers. We continued for two more weeks taking a course in radar.

Bring him home sooner...
Join the WAVES

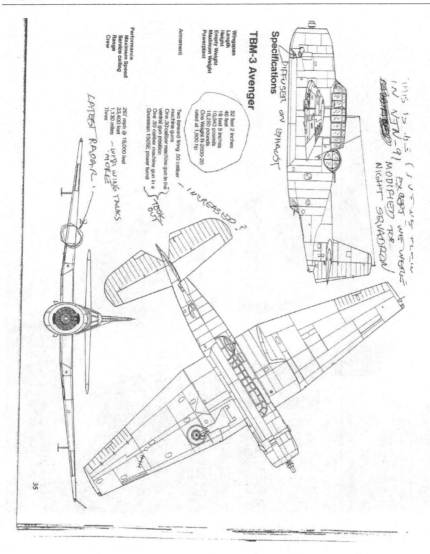

Specifications

TBM-3 Avenger

Wingspan	52 feet 2 inches
Length	40 feet
Height	16 feet 5 inches
Empty Weight	10,843 pounds
Maximum Weight	18,250 pounds
Powerplant	One Wright R-2600-20 rated at 1,900 hp
Armament	Two forward firing .50 caliber machine guns
	One .30 caliber machine gun in the ventral gun position
	One .50 caliber machine gun in a Grumman 150SE power turret
Performance	
Maximum Speed	267 mph @ 16,000 feet
Service ceiling	23,400 feet
Range	1,130 miles
Crew	Three

Handwritten notes:
- DIFFUSER ON EXHAUST
- THIS IS THE (TYPE WE FLEW) IN VTN-91 EXCEPT WE WERE MODIFIED FOR NIGHT SQUADRON
- INCREASED? → TOOK OUT
- LATEST RADAR.
- WING TANKS — MORE

Chapter 3 *Gunnery School*

Our next assignment was aerial gunnery school in Hollywood, Florida, at a boys' military school that the Navy had taken over. We had a good time there. Two other fellows and I shared a corner room on the second floor overlooking the tennis courts. One of the guys broke his collar bone the first week in Jujitsu class and had to drop out.

The first thing we did was learn to shoot skeet. The Navy always listed people alphabetically, which meant I was always first or second on any list. So, I was put up to shoot first with twenty-five shots. To start, we took the easiest position with the clay pigeon going straight out. I had only shot a shot gun three or four times in my life. I hollered, "Pull!" and the clay pigeon went flying out before me. I got a bead on it and followed its path until I was just ahead of it, then I squeezed the trigger without jerking. The clay pigeon burst into a puff of smoke. I had hit it dead center. This surprised me. So, I reasoned, '*All I have to do is, do it twenty-four more times.*' I didn't hit all of them dead center, but I got them all. I heard a boy behind me. who was from Brooklyn, whisper, "That's that boy from Tennessee."

We all learned to shoot from all positions. We then moved to 30 and 50 caliber machine guns. We shot at nylon sleeves on a moving rail car.

The tips of the bullets were dipped in paint and each person had a different color. When your bullet hit the sleeve, it left your color around the hole. At the end of a shoot, the scores were counted. We went through the school in sections of six or eight people. Several guys in my section, like me, could shoot above the average, so when we left the school, our sleeve was flying below he American flag at the base. This meant we had broken the record set by all previous classes.

We also had a lot of class work studying mathematics of trajectories of bullets. We also spent many hours in an aerial gunnery simulator. It was a regular gun turret that made noise and fired a beam of light. Before us was a screen with two projectors timed together to simulate enemy planes making passes on us at different angles. It also recorded our hits. WAVES ran the projectors, so when we weren't in the turret, we talked to the WAVE.

Chapter 4   *Flight Training*

After gunnery school we moved south a few miles to Miami
Naval Air Station to take flight training.

We began to fly out over the Atlantic in what is called today
the Bermuda triangle, but it didn't have a name then. We practiced
aerial gunnery, plane to flying sleeve, all kind of positions and
angles. We shot up old half sunken ships. We learned to dive bomb
at an angle of 60 degrees off the horizontal. We came in low over the
Everglades on our landing approach. We flew down Miami beach at
25 feet altitude using our radio altimeter. We would scare the day
lights out of people lying on the beach. We flew with different pilots
because we were testing each other. When we graduated we formed
permanent crews. I told my pilot I didn't want to be a dead hero. We
agreed.

At first, we flew old TBMs in flight school, but we later got the new torpedo plane, TBM-3 Avenger. which required a three-man crew. It had one 1900 horsepower radial engine, a wing span of 52 feet 2 inches, and a length of 40 fee with a maximum air speed of 267 mph and a range of 1,130 miles without wing tanks. With wing tanks the Avenger could fly another five or six hundred miles. Since it did not have diving flaps, 60 degrees was about as steep as it could safely dive. Most dives start out about 8,000 feet and the pull out begins at about 1500 feet just after the bomb is released. At the pull out, several "G" s of gravity are put on your body. About the time you are in horizontal position of 1300 feet, you feel the concussion from the bomb you have just dropped. If you go too low, the blast will down your plane.

One time in flight school we were going out to practice dive bombing with several other planes. Some of the planes had already taken off and others were taxing out to take off. My pilot was already in the plane waiting for me. I was delayed for some reason. I still looked the plane over, as a habit, before getting in even if I was late. This upset the pilot because that was his job. We were flying some old planes that had cloth covered elevators. The new planes we got later were all aluminum. I noticed something had hit one of the elevators and ripped a tear in two directions. The pilot had the engine running and I walked around in front and gave the signal to cut the engine. He cut the engine and jumped off the wing mad as a hornet. I motioned for him to follow me and pointed at the tear. Boy! Did his attitude change! I didn't say a word. He was sure glad I found it, but he didn't say so. The elevators are what pull out of a dive. Needless to say, I didn't choose him to be my pilot.

In training we dropped a lot of torpedoes that were set to run under the ships and later surface to be reclaimed. This was expensive. So, it was our lot to test a dummy torpedo made with 2,000 pounds of concrete. It was a long round block of concrete with eye hooks to attach it to the bombing shackles. We rendezvoused with one our ships way out in the Caribbean. We radioed in for permission to make our run. They were set to measure our distance, angle, altitude and speed. From this they could tell if we made a hit. The day was beautiful, not a cloud, and, it seemed, all the sailors on the ship were on deck to watch.

We started our run on a low angle, picking up speed as we descended to about 25 feet over the water. On radar, I had the ship's blip coming right down the middle of my screen. At 2,000 yards, I started counting backwards every 100 yards. At 1,000 yards, we were supposed to drop the fake bomb, but it wouldn't release. I hollered in my mike, "It's still in there!" My pilot started bouncing the plane and I kept on hollering, "It's still in there!" Finally, it let go, but by this time we were almost on top of the ship. I looked down real quick, just in time to see a big splash real close to the ship with all the sailors on deck. That was the end of concrete torpedoes.

My first bad experience occurred one day about half way between Miami and the Bahamas. We were flying formation and were switching to a different type formation when two of the planes collided. One broke in two and fell into the sea. The other went into a steep spiral spin. One chute came out just before it hit the water. Five men were lost as everybody looked on. One of the radiomen was my close friend. Since his bunk was next to mine, I was given the task of opening his locker and putting all his personal belongings in a box to send home.

Several days later, in almost the same place, doing the same thing, one of our planes come in behind us and chewed up our tail. The plane began shaking hard and my pilot ordered me to standby for bail out. The plane kept on flying in spite of the shaking, but we stuck with it and made it back.

★ ★ ★

Another time we had to rendezvous with a ship in the Caribbean that was dragging a sled which was intended to be a moving target for bombing practice. The problem was, we had drawn a real old plane, I mean, *antique,* and the radio transmitter was something I had never seen before. It had banks of coils mounted all around the bulkhead that plugged into the transmitter. I had to figure out which coils to use to get the frequency we needed. We had to use a certain frequency to call the ship.

We couldn't start bombing the sled without communicating and getting permission. I found a chart on the side of the transmitter that told me what coil to use. I plugged it in and set up the transmitter. I called the ship and said, "How do you read?"

They came back with, "Read you loud and clear." I was proud of myself.

Finally, it was graduation time again. We all received our wings. Air crew wings were sterling silver with a gold anchor in the center. Just above the wings was a place to attach gold battle stars. I received three battle stars while overseas for the battle of the Philippines, Okinawa, and Japan. The pilot and crewman I joined up with were Ensign A. D. Ridley, nicknamed Rip, and 3rd. class aviation mechanic, Allen Phinney. We stayed together for the rest of the war.

.

Chapter 5 *Training at various places*

After a week's leave and a short stay at Norfolk and Lowell, Massachusetts, I arrived at Quonset Point, Rhode Island. We formed a night squadron, VTN 91 and began heavy training around the clock.

Everything had to be practiced to perfection, but unexpected accidents happen. We were totally surprised one practice day during landing when our right tire blew out. We veered off the runway, hit soft dirt, and hung on as the plane came to rest with its nose in the ground. Only the pilot and I were on the plane and neither of us were hurt. I opened the door to see a lot of emergency vehicles bearing down on us at full speed. As I swung down from my door, someone grabbed my legs and helped me down safely.

We went to town on the weekends, mostly to Providence, Rhode Island. Regular sailors sometimes called us Airedales. We got the "Flight skins" or fifty percent over our base pay wo we usually had a little more money in our pockets. One day in town, another guy and I walked into a place and saw two sailors trying to pick up girls. When they saw us and our wings, one of the sailors said, "Here comes some damned Airedales. They got all the money and all the women!" We all laughed, but of course, it wasn't true.

One exciting thing we did was fly down to New York City around the Empire State Building and then head back. Some of the things we did are not allowed today, like flying three or four planes abreast so close to the water that we could see the planes next to us sucking up a whirlpool of water under their props. We knew our plane was doing the same thing although we couldn't see it.

Flying flat on the water, we would come up on little New England towns and pull up at the docks at the last second. On the ground, the people couldn't hear the engines until we were right on them. Thankfully those Americans showed a lot of tolerance of their Navy.

Several times, the table were turned, and I was woke up in the middle of the night by our own planes dive bombing our barracks and pulling out right over us one at a time. Everybody in bed was swearing, "Just wait, we'll get even!"
We also used to practice touch and go landings to a little spot marked out to simulate a carrier deck. On Saturday and Sunday evenings, when we did this, rows of cars would be parked just outside the fence watching the show. We turned out to be good entertainment for courting couples.

After a while our squadron was transferred to Boka Cheka Naval Air Station, Key West, Florida. We flew down stopping at Norfolk, Jacksonville, and Miami. We arrived at Norfolk at night. The Naval Air Station was near the municipal airport. One of our planes landed at the municipal airport while taking instruction from the Navy tower. Were they embarrassed!

We flew out of Norfolk with one other plane. About thirty minutes out at about 3000 feet altitude, we skimmed along over heavy clouds as far as we could see. Something zoomed by us at great speed! As we tried to figure out what it was, a F40 fighter (Corsair) popped up out of the clouds. We now knew what had happened. We had talked with a F40 pilot just before we left

Norfolk. He had made a pass on us out of the sun showing he wanted to play. We spent thirty minutes trying to out maneuver him. When we came to North Miami Beach we followed the other plane down. He went in over some houses and palm trees to about twenty-five feet off the beach. He shook the palm trees and we were right behind him. If a pilot did that today, he would be put in *jail*.

While we were at Key West, we worked hard. This was a test for endurance with minimum ground support. We flew around the clock, sometimes three flights a day. With briefing and debriefing, a flight lasted four or six hours. We had about four hours between flights. The squadron had received new airplanes made by General Motors and we had to test them. This included stalling them out and doing maneuvers that put a strain on the plane. Some of the engines began to cut out and we lost several planes in the drink. If the plane fell in shallow water, they were floated back to surface and reclaimed. At least one radioman didn't survive a crash due to engine trouble. The cause of the engine failure turned out to be a faulty carburetor.

We flew long flights over Cuba. I remember coming back one Saturday night over Havana I picked up the Grand Old Opera on the radio. On another night, when we got caught in a severe storm and one plane got lost and two other planes tried to land at the same time. One plane came down to top of the other, but no one was injured. It would have been hard to believe but the dents on the bottom of the wings were visible as proof.

Another tragedy happened one night when one of our planes two didn't pull out of a dive soon enough. The radioman tried to bail out, but he hit the water before his chute opened. The pilot rode the plane down and leveled off on a deserted island, knocking down a path of scrub oaks. When his plane came to a stop, there were no wings or tail left, but the pilot was safe. The next morning, he found his radioman floating in the surf with his chute open. A radioman went on all the flights, but the third crewman did not, which is why there were only two aboard the plane.

The radioman who died had no living kin and he had requested a military funeral. For some reason unknown to me, I was asked to look after his funeral. We buried him in a Key West cemetery.

We did a lot of stupid but fun things, like chasing sharks in the shallow water with the airplane and laying down a row of machine gun bullets across it.

We island hopped small uninhabited islands in the Bahamas about a low as we could go. Once as we crossed one of the islands very low, we came suddenly upon a mast of a sailing ship tied up in a bay. As I looked down I could see the planking of the deck, and as I looked back, there stood a man with his feet wide apart shaking both fists at us. We probably scared the daylights out of him. We hadn't done it on purpose, but I know he thought we did.

One day as soon as we took off, we had an emergency. My pilot couldn't see out his windshield. We had a dumb ensign over the ground crew who ordered his crew to paint the props with a coat of oil to protect them from the weather. By the time we reached the end of the runway, the oil had come back in a fine mist and covered the canopy. We made it back around and landed with difficulty. My pilot chewed out the ground officer.

TBM-3 Avenger

Chaptere 6 *Last stage of training*

Our next move was back up the east coast to Martha's Vineyard, an island off Cape Cod. It was about the first of February and very cold. When we got to Norfolk, the ocean was frozen along the coast. Our plane didn't have heaters and it wasn't air tight. Our other crewman went by train, but another pilot, Tanner, was in the back with me. When we stopped at Norfolk, Tanner got out a fifth of whiskey and some blankets. I didn't drink but I took some to try to stay warm as we flew the rest of the way.

When we landed as Quonset Point on a snow-covered runway, my feet were so numb I could not feel the ground I was standing on. I finally got warm with no frost bite. When we got to Martha's Vineyard, we were issued fleece lined boots, pants and jackets. We had to blow hot air for about thirty minutes on the engines before they would start. We flew long-distance flights north. We still didn't have heaters in the back, but the pilot got heat from the engines.

Lucius Agee

One cold dark night, several miles north of the island, we were practicing dive bombing with six or seven other planes. As the custom was, we would drop a smoke light in the water and use that as a target. All our planes had one light on the top of their vertical stabilizer. As we looked out, all we could see in the black were single lights moving in a circle as each climbed to an altitude of about 8,000 feet. Being a night squadron, we had special diffusers over the exhaust pipes, so no one could see the exhaust flames.

As each plane started their dive, the light seemed to pause and then descend fast at a sixty-degree angle. The practice was to give your call sign and say "taps" when you started your dive and say "reveille" when you pulled out. One plane said taps and we watch as his light went down. Then all at once at the bottom of his dive his light went out and nothing but silence came on the radio. We all knew. Three men were lost. Nobody said anything on the radio for a long time.

One Friday afternoon we were given the weekend off. But we had a problem. No transportation was available. The ferry was iced in and no planes were flying. There were only two little towns on the island, so we wanted to go to the mainland.

Two or three other guys and I went to the docks and talked a fisherman into taking us to the mainland for a fee. It was cold and about fifteen miles of open sea to the mainland. His boat was a small inboard fishing boat. We went below and stood around the engine to get the heat off the engine and to get out of the wind.

We came in sight of land but also in sight of ice about a half mile from shore. The ice shelf was thin on the outward edge but thicker toward shore. A big ship had been through the ice a short time before us because the ice was cracked in big pieces. Our fisherman put the bow of his boat very gently against the ice. Then he opened up the throttle for several minutes. It didn't look like we were doing anything. He then let his throttle off and waited. Soon a huge piece of ice, maybe two or three hundred feet long, began to float away from the mainland ice. Before long we had a channel of clear water.

We saw cars on the mainland and decided to get off anywhere we could. He found some solid ice that was safe to stand on and we got out with maybe one hundred yards to land. We hitch hiked into the next town and caught a train to Providence.

Atop the Peabody Hotel, Memphis, Tennessee, dinner and big band were enjoyed by our crew and friends.

Chapter 7 *Preparing to go to war*.

The word was given, one weeks leave and then overseas. Trains were the way most people traveled. I decided to go home even though it meant I would have only twenty-four hours at home and required riding the trains twenty-four hours a day. I shared part of my train ride to Nashville with a radioman, Bret Hargest, who was going home to Jonesboro, Arkansas. He split off at Cincinnati.

Later overseas, when he was taking off a ship, the catapult malfunctioned and his plane went into the water. All three crewmen got off and were talking to each other as the ship went by. It was at night and they were too close to the ship. Pushing the ship were four large screws along at twenty-four knots causing a wake of over a mile long. Only one was found and it wasn't him. He had signed my scrap book earlier with the words, "Remember the ride to Cincinnati".

When we got back from leave, we were put on a special train for San Diego. When we got there, they sent us to a Boot Camp instead of putting us on a ship. There had been an accident on the ship and it had to be repaired.

We had to choose between going on leave for a week or staying at Boot Camp. Of course, we all headed for San Diego, even though most of us didn't have much money since we had spent it all on the east coast.

I went on leave with Jerry Highland and, between us, we had nineteen dollars. Sailors call San Diego, just Diego. When we got there, we had nowhere to sleep. Every USO, hotel, YMCA was full. The movie theaters stayed open around the clock so people could sleep there. Some hotels would let us sleep in the chairs in the lobby but not on the floor. We went back to the YMCA to use the bath room which was down a long hall and down stairs. The hall was six feet wide with little white hexagonal tile on the floor. We stepped over all these people going to the rest room and there were a lot of people going. One guy was lying in the window sill in the rest room.

On our first night we met two girls at a carnival. We spent a lot of money riding little cars that bump together. It was rare to meet two girls with so many sailors in town. We rode with them on the public bus and said good night and they got off. We stayed on the bus until it got back to town. I found a good place to sleep that no one else had discovered. We went in one of the nice hotels and all the chairs were full. I noticed one of the large couches had some space between it and the wall down at the floor. When no one was looking, I slid myself in. It was nice and private with plush carpet.

By the middle of the week we were just about out of money and spent our day at Balboa Park watching the animals and eating cinnamon rolls from a brown bag. At night we walked the streets like all the other sailors. While walking in front of a large grocery store with an open front and no doors, I noticed something on the sidewalk. I picked it up and saw it was money! I started walking faster expecting someone to tap me on the shoulder. I turned the corner and my buddy came running up to see what was wrong. With both hands, I help up the fifty-dollar bill! We went immediately and got us a steak dinner.

Chapter 8 *On to Hawaii*

We were sent by ship to Pearl Harbor. We were station This was about the first of March 1945. We continued to train on all types of flights. We enjoyed going into Honolulu on a little narrow gage steam engine train. I tried my hand at surfing at Waikiki.

Our fighter squadron soon joined us there. They flew F6F's, known as the Hellcat. This was a busy airfield with a lot of other activity besides our air group. I saw one man burned up in an air crash and another dove into the side of a mountain to crash. Big black smoke rose up in a column. They were not in our air group.

We had the latest radar and were doing a lot of unusual things. One night we took off on a training mission toward our target, a little uninhabited island on the east side of the big island. The plan was to come in low over the big island between two mountain peaks. The training was for me to tell the pilot every move to make as soon as we were airborne using my radar for information.

I took us around Diamond Head and down the west side of Maliki and Maui and the big island, Hawaii, to the city of Hilo. There I turned almost 90 degrees straight across between the two mountain peaks. The mountain peaks were 13,000 feet above sea level and the valley between was about 6,000 feet above sea level. I had never flown over this in the day time. We set an altitude just a little above the lowest point. Radar does not give a good return over land, so I had to sweat it out to get it right. After a few minutes, I was very relieved to see water on my radar screen which meant we had a clear shot to the water on the other side.

We regularly went swimming at the beach on the north side of the island. We had the use of a two-ton truck which we often parked by bumping it gently into a palm tree. Sometimes a coconut would fall out. Usually we were the only people there except for natives who were sometimes on the beach playing guitars.

The waves were huge and dangerous. One of our guys got knocked out when a wave slammed him down on the beach. Someone got him by the hair and pulled his face out of the water.

We used a one-man raft to float out beyond the breakers. Once I was out there sunning and looked up to realize I was out too far. I started paddling for shore but found I was in trouble. The current was going out and my paddling as hard as I could only kept me at the same distance from shore with huge boulders with a side drift. To my side was a rocky point with waves splashing against the rocks. I wanted help, but my buddies had gone with the natives somewhere and nobody was on the beach. I was on my own. The only thing I could do was keep paddling and drift into the rocks. It was dangerous but so was drifting out to sea with no clothes or water. When I got closer to the rocks, I slid out of the raft and it went flying in the surf. I held on to boulders and made my way from boulder to boulder between the waves. I got to shore and thanked God! I had learned a lesson the hard way.

★ ★ ★

On another night, we flew a formation of four or five planes east of Barbers' Point for about two hundred miles in a search pattern. On our farthest leg. I reported a ship at a certain bearing, thirty miles out. When we got back to base no one else had seen the ship. They started kidding me and saying I had probably see a rain squall. After the bombing of Pearl Harbor, there were strict regulations to check out every citing that was not identified. After checking with command center, we were told that no ships were known to be in that area. The office in charge came back to me and said, "Are you sure? No one else saw it. It's not supposed to be there. If we turn it in and they go to a lot of trouble to check it out and find nothing, we are going to look bad."

I said, "I'm sorry, but I got to report what I saw. I saw a ship." Later that day, word came. I was right. There was a ship that had left Pearl Harbor without giving proper departure information.

Another dark night, as we came back from a flight, we flew over Honolulu at about 8,000 feet altitude. All at once, brighter than day light, we were in cross lights of many high-powered search lights. It was a prearranged test. We tried every maneuver we could but could not lose them.

On a day time practice, we were instructed in a survival class to put on our flight suits with parachute harness and a one-man seat pack. They put us in a PT boat and hauled us out to sea beyond the sight of land. They said, "This is a test. Nobody knows it is not real but us. Try to signal ships or planes." With the PT boat running full throttle, we rolled off the side. After a rough entry into the water, we had to inflate our May West Vest and get the one-man raft out of the seat pack, inflate it and get in without losing any of the survival material in the pack. Next, we had to get together and tie the rafts together, put sun burn screen on our faces and feet, and check out our signaling devices. Some didn't use the cream and got severely burned, especially on the feet. Some lost the material in their packs. We put yellow dye in the water as shark repellent.

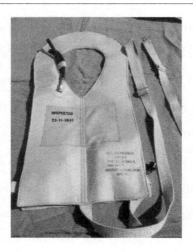

We were in the water from about eight in the morning until three in the afternoon before we were able to get the attention of a B26. Someone shot a Ferris Pistol (rocket flare). The plane turned and came over us rocking its wings. Next came a Piper Cub with a big red cross on it. We now knew we would be picked up shortly, so someone said, "Let's go swimming." It sounded like a good idea since it was hot, so most of us peeled off our clothes and went in. We started splashing around and some rafts got turned over. I saw the ship coming and got on my clothes pretty quick. I was the first man to climb up the cargo net they had thrown over the side. Just as I was coming aboard, one of the ship's crew hollered, "Sharks!" I thought he was kidding, but as I turned around, there were six or seven huge sharks cruising in and around the rafts. The sharks were longer than the rafts. Everybody moved quickly and got aboard the ship. All the noise and splashing had brought the sharks in. They swam right through the dye. We learned what not to do, and '*the dye don't work*'

Another officer joined our squadron in the Hawaiian Islands who was supposed to be a radar expert. He wes a political appointee with the rank of Lr. Commander. Shame on the Navy and Congress. There was not a radioman in our squadron who did not know more than him. He flew with me one time to give instuctions. We flew down to the big island and back. As we were coming up on Moloki, two large blips showed up on the radar screen. He quickly jumped to a conclusion and pointed out to me the first one Moloki and the second one was Maui. I shook my head NO and said that wasn't right. He began to get angry and I saw there was no reasoning with him, so I climbed in the empty turret and left him alone.

Not only was he dumb and hard headed, he had no common sense. What he was seeing was two hills on Moloki with skip distance in between. A little mental calculation of your milage maps and radar screen would confirm this. After leaving Molaki, we were over open water for several minutes before Maui came up on the horizon. I got his attention and pointed to the horizon. I don't know if he figured it out or not. He became the squadron joke.

Later, when we were on the ship, he went up with one of the planes as an observer and had no duties. He was in the empty turret and was going to be catapulted off. It was in the day time and, as usual, a lot of people were on the island watching. He was busy watching the people instead of looking after business.

To catapult off, the pilot runs the engine up until it is trying to jump off the deck. If the engine is running correctly, the pilot signals a deck hand who is holding a raised flag. The deck hand drops the flag and this is the signal to catapult. The crewman on board must listen to the engine and keep an eye on the flagman. When the flag drops, the crewman knows the plane is going to catapult immediately. The new guy was so busy watching the people watch him that he forgot to buckle his seat belt and shoulder harness. He had no idea when he would be shot off. When he was, there was laughter from everybod on the island! The last thing everybody saw was his face plastered up against the inside of the plexiglass turret.

The last insult to our squadron was when they passed out metals. This was done on our way back to the states on the flight deck. We were all in formation. When they called out his name and the metal he didn't deserve, a groan went up from the ranks.

Rescue plane

r

Chapter 9 *Into the fight*

The word came that the "Franklin" was coming into Pearl. It was all shot up from kamikazi attacks.The Franklin was a new essex class aircraft carrier. People we had trained with had made up its air group and it had lost a lot of it's crew. We were on the docks when it came in. It is a wonder it made its way back under its own power. The island was a rusty hulk of iron and all the elevators were tilted in their hold. In many places we could see daylight through the hanger deck. None of the air group was left on the ship. No one said it, but we all wondered what was in store for us.

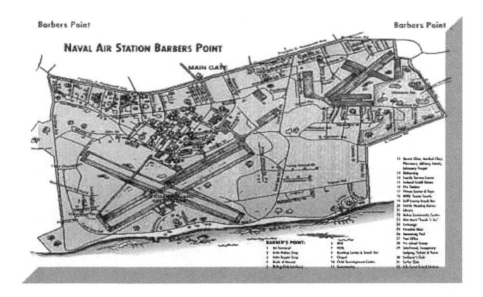

Aircraft carrier USS *Franklin* (CV-13) attacked during World War II, March 19, 1945. Photographed by PHC Albert Bullock from the cruiser USS *Santa Fe* (CL-60), which was alongside assisting with firefighting and rescue work. Photo #: 80-G-273880, Official U.S. Navy Photograph

If I had decided not to joined the night squadron, I would have been on this ship.

We went aboard the essex class air craft carrier the Bon Homme Richard CV31 about the first of April, 1945.

The essex class carrier was the newest and biggest we had. It had a maximum speed of of 33 knots. On our shake down cruise, the pilots went up by themselves to practice carrier landings. I bet they blew out a dozen tires the first day. They soon learned how to land at night with very little light. Our landing lights were, you might say, homemade. There were, I guess, four on each side, made with one half inch pipe elbows. They were embeded in the deck with only the round part protruding above the deck. A small peanut light was down in the pipe. It could only be seen from the side and only by the plane in the groove. The pilot found its way back to the ship by coded radar. Once over the ship, the pilot might be able to see the ship or not, depending on the moon and clouds.

The thing that a plane would depend on seeing was the wake of the ship. There was fluoresence in the water and the ships wake made it glow. The pilot could always see a flourescence streak. The LSO (landing signal officer) had a flourescent suit that picked up the glow from the wake. But he couldn't help you if he couldn't see the plane. Our planes were painted blue black and the exhaust flames were hidden and we had on no lights. No one was allowed to smoke on deck. I believe VTN 90 on the Enterprise and our VTN 91 were the first carrier based night squadrons. Our air group consisted of a squadron of TBM Avengers and a squadron of F6F Hellcats.

Air groups on carriers are considered guests on the ship. That means, the air groups had no ship duties but we did have squadron duties.

On my first carrier night flight, I was unprepared for the darkness. When I stepped out on the flight deck, I did not have night vison and couldn't see my hand in front of my face. I could hear those big radial engines turning over everywhere. I got a deck hand to lead me to my plane. Later we wore red goggles for thirty minutes before each flight.

We left Pearl to join the third fleet off Okinawa with a short stop at Ulithi. During this period, we flew patrol flights in all kind of weather. Tokyo Rose broadcast we would be sunk.

A squadron of carrier planes could land quick. We trained for this. Say, a group of planes fixing to land would fly upwind in formation over the ship. At a certain distance out, each plane would peel off to the left into the crosswind one at a time. All planes made a rectangular path to the flight deck. Upwind, peel off into crosswind, downwind and crosswind, into upwind to land. When we turned into the second crosswind, we could see the ship on the right traveling about 24 knots, at 90 degrees to our plane. By the time we got into position, the ship would pass to the left. We then turned tight to the left to be in the groove for landing. As we landed, our tail hook caught and our wheels made a cry as they suddenly began to rotate. A deck hand made a dash to unhook the plane. In seconds, we moved up behind the barrier cables. About this time, we heard the wheel cry of the next plane landing behind us. This continued until all the planes were on board.

Chapter 10 *Bombing missions*

One of my first bombing missions over Japan was with several other planes. It was at night. We dropped aluminum chaft all the way in to jam the enemy radar. Phenney poked it out the turret window as I handed it up to him. When our planes were converted to night flight, all guns were removed from the rear as they would give away our position. For this reason, Phenney didn't always go

One day on a patrol flight, we came up on one of the Jap held islands which the Navy had bypassed. It looked so peaceful until I saw a Japanese Zero coming up. We were no match for a Zero. The Zero came up along side us just out of gunnery range. After a few minutes, we made a wide turn back toward our ship. The Zero did not attack. His orders were probably to defend only.

Once when it was almost dark, one of the other carriers had an emergency and sent a F4Y fighter to land on our ship. I was on the catwalk just off the flight deck with some others watching because he had already taken two wave-offs. As he came around on this third attempt, we all knew he was too low and the LSO gave him another wave-off. He poured on the gas as he came in over the deck trying to gain altitude. Just beyond the arresting cables were about three barrier cables. They swung with hydraulics to about four feet. Hitting them was about like hitting a rock wall. The F4U's wheels were down too low to miss them. The men operating the cables could see this, and there were no planes beyond the cables, so they started dropping the cables. The first two dropped, but the third man wasn't fast enough. The F4U's wheels caught the cable and he flipped slammed on the deck. A crane ran over and picked up the plane and the pilot got out and walked away. They dropped the plane overboard.

☆ ☆ ☆

With all the night flying, we became familiar with the night sky. I use to practice guessing at our bearing using the North Star and time observing the the position of the Big Dipper. Then I would check my compass and watch. I didn't miss much.

When the amphibious landing was made in Okinawa, I flew in a circle just off the shore. Our plane was used as a radio relay. There were no enemy aircraft. I thought the landing was the first but it wasn't.

We were in a big storm and, I believe, one destroyer was sunk. We always had a destroyer off our port side. In rough seas a destroyer was tossed with one end actually leaving the water. I have seen two thirds daylight under the hull.

Every now and then, we would meet a tanker to refuel. This was done with the tanker running on our starboard side, with, I guess, about twenty feet between us, depending on how rough the sea was. Some other ship would come up on the other side of the tanker and we would be traveling side by side at about twenty knots. They would shoot over a small line that would bring over the large ropes. The fuel line swung out on booms.

Sometimes, we would refuel a smaller ship. On several occasions we refueled an English ship. We sure envied those sailors because they wore shorts. Sometimes we transferred food, like beans. The wind and noise from the water prevented us from talking back and forth.

The fleet was attacked several times by kamikaze planes. When all the five inch guns were firing the noise echoed through out the ship. We could also hear the 40 and 20 MM guns. We had one splash close to us. Our fighter pilots shot down several. Ensign McDonald shot down four and one probable in one flight.

For security reasons we were not allowed to have camera. We had one official squadron photographer. One of our radioman, however, had one at the risk of being court marshalled. Nobody knew about it until he was reported missing in action. They found it in his locker. One of his close friends told of something he did. When we were under attack by kamakazi planes, the ship was on general quarters and he was supposed to be in his quarters. Instead he crawled through one of the large air vents that went to the outside and took pictures from there.

On day flights, we usually flew off and catapulted off at night. So one day, on a mission over Japan, we flew off loaded with bombs and two auxillary fuel tanks on our wings to extend our range. We were loaded so heavy when we left the ship, we dropped altitude until we were close to the water. As I looked at the water, I saw a long row of little splashes just below our plane. For an instant, this gave me a bad scare because it looked like machine gun bullets. Then I realized it was a school of flying fish.

We had a bulletin board where flights were posted. One time I was posted for a flight over Japan on Friday the 13th, in plane 13, at one in the morning. In military time, 1:00 P. M. is 1300 hours. All day people kept slapping me on the back, saying how nice it was to have known me. I was lucky. I didn't have any trouble on the flight.

I had a good, new, fluffy, cotton mattress. Every so often, we would sun our mattressses. It was usually on a nice sunny day when we were not in danger. Each group had a certain time to sun. One day after sunning my mattress, I went to get it and someone had stolen it and left me an old slick mattress made with wood excelser. It was too knotty to sleep on. That night I just slept on my canvas bunk.

The next day, another group took their mattresses out. I took the old mattress and put it out just like one of them. I found me a nice fluffy mattress with no name on it. I took it down to my bunk and got out my indelible ink and, with an old tooth brush, wrote AGEE all over it in big letters. It was so bad, nobody would want to steal it.

That's called survival at sea.

☆ ☆ ☆

Somebody was always saying how glad they would be to get to go home. It was common for guys to say they were going to do something crazy and get out on a Section 8. Most all were just kidding. If someone went berserk or out of his mind, he would probably be discharged according to Section 8 of military law. There was one guy in our squadron who ws always doing this. His name of Loeffler, nicknamed Lucky, from Milwaukee. One day when I was in the ready room, someone came in and said, "Lucky is in the sick bay. He's gone nuts."

I said, "Oh, come on. He's putting on, you know." Word came later. They didn't think he was faking. They thought it was the result of a crash landing back in the states. Anyway, they sent him back. When we got back to San Francisco after the war, he met us at the dock. He had made 1st. class petty officer. All our ranks were frozen and had been for a long time. We were still 3rd. class petty officers.

I still don't know if he was faking or not.

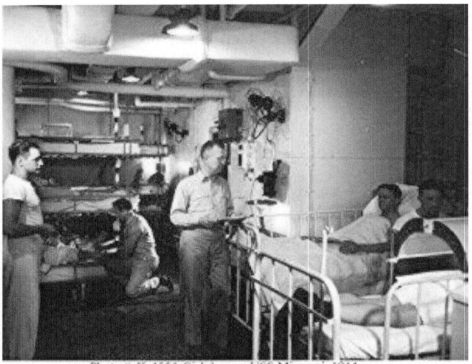

Photo # K-4554 Sick bay on USS Missouri, 1944

Chapter 11 *More battles*

While in the chow line one night, one of our squadron crewmen came running in and said, "Agee! They got a sub spotted. You and Rip are going after it!" I ran to the ready room and the intelligence officer briefed me on all the codes of the day as I put on my flight suit. We ran to the plane which was already on the catapult with the engine running. In just a few minutes from the chow line, I was being catapulted into the dark night. I quickly picked up the sub on my radar. There were a hundred or more ships spread out over thirty miles and the sub had popped up in the middle. A ship and a surfaced sub look the same on radar. I had to be sure. If we went straight for the sub and they picked us up on radar, they would submerge before we could get there. I told Rip, "Let's take a course about 15 degrees off and an altitude of 300 feet." He agreed and when we got to the lowest point, we made a sharp 90 degree turn and came in low and fast. The sub was still there. We dropped a depth charge 25 feet off the water right on top of it. It was black outside so I couldn't see a thing. I have often wondered how much damage we did.

Our pilots drew names to see who got to fly to Guam to pick up mail for our ship. Rip won. When we got to Guam and landed, he was accustomed to having a hook catch us so he didn't touch a brake, and over the intercom said, "Roll, dam you, roll." I thought we would never stop rolling

After parking we started up the hill toward a canteen to get something to eat and see some girls. The WAVEs were there. Before we got there two Shore Patrols came and chewed us out because we didn't have on the the uniform of the day. We had our flight suits on but we couldn't talk them into letting us go on. We went to the officer's club but I couldn't go in. Rip went in and got us a drink and a sandwich and we sat a the picnic table outside.

We went back and reported the *chicken manure.* Everybody agreed, just like the Navy.

★ ★ ★

Underneath the flight deck hanging over the water was a catwalk made with pipe and expanded metal. We used this as a short cut to the ready room. It was narrow and inconvenient so was seldom used by the ship's crew. Early one morning just at daylight, I was on my way to the ready room when I saw someone in the distance wearing a foul weather jacket that he didn't need. I thought I recognized him, and when he saw me, he took off in the opposite direction. I said to myself, "He's up to something" so I ran him down. When he saw he was caught, he turned and showed me what he was doing. He opened his foul weather jacket and under his arm was a large jar of homemade peach brandy. He and one of the cooks had made it. I took a taste and he went on to his hiding place. He was one of the squadron crewmen.

It was hot in our sleeping quarters and cool on the flight deck. With the ship movement, we had a cool breeze all the time, Our ready room was airconditioned and we stayed there a lot. One night, I took my mattress up on the flight deck. I was sleeping good when all of a sudden we were right in the middle of a rain storm and I got soaking wet.

Not to be outdone, a few nights later, I took my mattress with its flash cover up on the catwalk under the flight deck. I tied myself down so I wouldn't fall off. Ever now and then, a spray of water would come up. It was cool and I went to sleep fast. Then, about 3:00 A. M. General Quarters sounded. I had to get up fast and run with my mattress to my quarters. After this, I gave up sleeping anywhere else.

The ship had to turn into the wind to launch and receive planes. The ship can turn sharp. It has something like wings to stabilize it. If a sailor was walking across the flight deck and it turned sharp, it would list over so far that he couldn't continue walking. He would have to reach down and hold on to the cleats in the deck.

One night after returning from a flight, I was going down the stairs from the side elevator to the catwalk that ran under the flight deck. No hand rail goes higher than the flight deck, so I had no hand rail. As I started down the stairs with my plotting board in my hands, the ship suddenly turned, listing sharply on my side. I fell with one leg hanging off the stairs. I grabbed steel and had to hold on in that same position for several minutes until the ship straightened up. It was dark; the ship was doing 24 knots; and it was 55 feet to the water. If I had fallen off, I would have been *long gone.*

Chapter 12 *Fun and flights*

We flew most of every day with about half of them being patrol flights. There were two ready rooms on board. One was the officer ready room but we all used it to put on our flight suits and gather our materials for flight. That was where we were briefed for the flight and debriefed after a mission. The other ready room was for enlisted men and had easy chairs and gave us a place to hang out.

One of the problems we had to contend with was boredom and lack of material to keep our minds busy. We had a wire recorder, a record player and a lot of records. We, the inlisted men, decided to produce a thirty minute radio program. Guys were named to be script writers, actors, sound effect makers, commercial makers, etc. We didn't keep the same job all the time, so I got to do various things.

The name of our program was *The Lone* The name of our program was *The LoneStranger*. We used the <u>William Tell Overture</u> from *The Lone Ranger* radio program as our theme song. One of the boys in our squadron cut hair, so the setting for our program was a barber shop run by him after the war. Different guys from our squadron would come in and soon would start telling of his war experience. We would usually blow it up, so it was about half true.

It would take about a week of our spare time to make a thirty-minute program. If someone had an unusual experience, he would get in the script. We used this to really get to the pilots and some of the officers.

In the script we could do anything. In the commercials, we would advertise something like women's underwear or some ridiculous thing. We played our program at a regular time each week. Pilots and crewmen would crowd into one ready room, standing room only. There was a lot of laughter and fun.

Sleeping quarters

I participated in two bombardments. One was in July on the Hitachi Engine Works north of Tokyo. We had several battle ships, plus the King George from Britian. I flew spotter over the target. It was at night. There was a gunnery officer from one of the battle ships in Phenney's seat on the radio calling the shots. I just watched. I could only hear the roar of our engine and all I could see was flashes of lights and fires. Photographers later showed we did a lot of damage.

One night while on sub patrol when we were returning on our last leg, a very bright light was shining about where our ship was supposed to be.This was very unusual because all ships ran dark. We kept wondering what could have happened. As we got closer the light went out and we landed safely. What had happened was this. One of the planes running with us landed on a carrier but his right wing hit the gun turret and it spun him around. As he spun, his left wing clipped somebody on deck and took both his legs off. It was pitch dark, The captain took a chance of being hit by a sub when he ordered the lights on.

Another night, one of our planes was overdue. We were on the catwalk just off the flight deck where the planes land. We were watching and listening and figuring how much time he had before his gas ran out. This was not the first time we had a plane go missing. Then we heard his plane and strained in the darkness to see him. The first thing we saw was the smoke coming from his engine. Then there he was in the groove. At this range we could see him good because the moon was out. The second he cut his engine, the prop and engine froze. He glided in without a sound. When the tail hook jerked him a stop and the engine plopped out on the deck. Fire fighters rushed over and prevented a fire. The crew was OK. They had taken a shell in the engine and mountings.

The fire fighters on our ship were very good. One time, one of our planes crashed into the five inch turrets. It spilled gasoline all over the rear elevator and the gasoline ran down the elevator well into the hanger deck. The gasoline was on fire and still pouring out. All around the elevator, in the hanger deck, were TBMs and F6Fs parked as close as we could get with folded wings and loaded with bombs. When I saw this, I ran to a hatch and went down to the deck below the hanger deck and then forward until I was well away from the area. There I sat and waited for the explosions that never came. Somehow they put it out.

: Point Ted Sub pick-up point

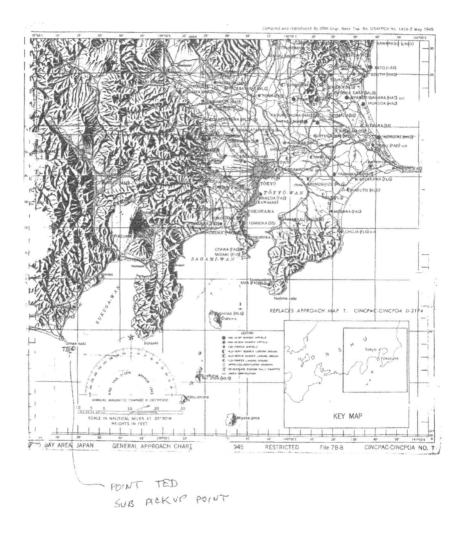

Point Blondie: Sub pick-up point

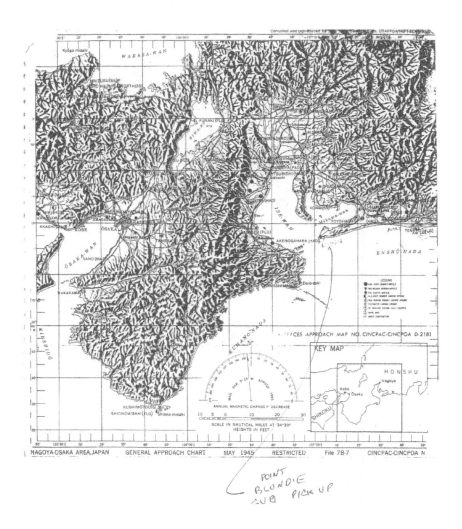

NAGOYA-OSAKA AREA,JAPAN   GENERAL APPROACH CHART   MAY 1945   RESTRICTED   File 7B-7   CINCPAC-CINCPOA N

POINT
BLONDIE
SUB PICK UP

Flight deck emergency personnel carrying fire extinguishers move in on a TBM-3 of VC-83 after it went into the barrier aboard USS SARGENT BAY (CVE-83) on 14 June 1945.(USN via David Lucabaugh)

The deck crew aboard USS ENTERPRISE (CV-6) disengages the tail hook of a TBM-3 of VT(N)-90 on 8 March 1945. The machine guns have been removed from the turret, and 'stinger' position. During this period ENTERPRISE was operating as a night carrier and VT(N)-90 was employed on night intruder missions. (USN via David Lucabaugh)

THIS IS THE SAME AS OUR SQUADRON VTN-91. WE WERE IN THE SAME TASK FORCE ALSO.

Chapter 13 *Heckler missions*

We began to fly a lot of night heckler missions. We would bomb, strafe (spray various targets with machine gun bullets) and shoot rockets on airfields. Only one plane would go to each field. This way if we saw planes on our radar, and we did, we knew to avoid them. We also had the Japs fooled at first. They thought we were friendly. We came in over their runway at 500 feet at, say, 3:00 in the morning, and being a single engine plane by himself, they couldn't believe we came from a carrier. We usually got a green blinker light from the tower, meaning clear to land. What we were doing was picking out what target we wanted to hit. We usually carried one incendiary bomb to drop first in order to start a fire. After the first bomb was dropped all lights would go out. Our plane carried 2,000 pounds of bombs, eight five inch rockets, plus our wing guns.

I had control of the bomb selector switches. One of our bombs was called "Butterfly Bomb". It was a canister with a lot of little bombs inside like an egg crate. It was dropped from about five hundred feet. When it hit the air, a drag on the tail would open the front. It would flutter like a butterfly, spreading little bombs all over. This is where we got our call sign, *egg crate three one three.*

All the other bombs were dropped by dive bombing. After the first pass, we knew they would be shooting back. The time I saw a tracer bullet, I thought, at first, it was sparks from our engine. When we fired our rockets or our machine gun, it gave our position away.We usually made our passes headed toward the sea. In case we were hit, we would try to make it to the designated point where a sub would pick us up. It usually took eight or more passes for us to empty our plane of ammunition and call the mission complete.

No alcohol was allowed on the ship, except a can of hot beer was given to each person returning from a combat mission. I did not like the hot beer, so I gave mine away. Boy, did I have a lot of friends!

One flight I remember very well because there were heavy clouds all the way to the target.We climbed above the clouds and it was bright moon light. The clouds looked like a big carpet of snow are far as we could see. It was my job to get us to the target. The difficult part was getting to the target which was about forty miles behind Mt. Fugi. Radar didn't work as well over land as over water and the bends in a river could cause a problem. Rip was a little surprised when we came down through the clouds and the target field was right there all lit up. Its name was Kofu.

In our ready room was a teletype machine. Messages were projected on a screen so everybody in the room could read it. We usually got *'well done'* messages if everything went well.

★ ★ ★

Early one morning we were sitting in our ready room waiting for our teletype machine to tell us to man our planes. It was raining and the wind was strong. No moon or stars in this kind of weather. The teletype came into action. Click, click -----cancel DUDCAP. DUDCAP means dusk until dawn ecombat air patrol. We started laughing because this suited us just fine. We could go back to bed. Just as we were leaving for our bunks, the teletype started up again. It was giving *a 'well done'* message for the planes that just landed. They had been operational with 55 knots of wind across the the deck.

When bombing the enemy air fields, it took a little time to climb to 8,000 feet and back over the target. By the time we made eight or more passes, we would have been over the target thirty minutes or more. This is plenty of time for enemy planes to come up after us.

It was dark and we knew they would have radar, but, I believe, we had *better* radar. Since we were by ourselves, any other plane we saw on the radar was unfriendly. We didn't have a lot trouble with planes that I know of, except for one night on our way back to the ship about ten miles out when three planes came in formation flying an intercept course with us. We held our course until we were real close to them. So close, we came that when we cut in behind them we lost them. We made our way back unharmed.

On Sunday we had church services. Our attendance was more than usual at this time. Most of us carried a New Testament in our knee pocket of our flight suit, but there was one guy in our squadron, a radioman named Weathorford, who carried a great big full Bible. It was about eight inches by eleven inches and the only way he could carry it was in his arms. With all his other gear, it was too much. We all knew this but no one dared say anything to him. One night he radioed in that they had spotted an enemy ship and were going to make a run on it. The was the last we ever heard from him. They were listed as mission in action.

One night returning from a heckler mission over Japan, I was watching the long distance radar. There before me were thirty miles of ships. We had a piece of electronic gear called 'IFF' (Identification Friend or Foe) which sent a coded signal. One of my jobs on each mission was to set the code of the day. As we got closer to the fleet, we heard on the radio command, "Bogey 280 degrees at five hundred feet". I looked at my altimeter and compass and came to attention quick…*it was us*! I called Rip, "Did you hear that?"

Rip said, "Yeah."

My pilot was in charge and I waited for him to decide what to do. He didn't decide fast enough to suit me, so I said, "We better break radio silence, hadn't we?"

He said, "Yeah."

I called in. *"Rover Boy, this is Egg Crate 3-1-3.* We are on a 280 degree heading at 500 feet, over."

They came back with "Egg Crate 3-1-3, make a 180 degree turn, fly for ten minutes, then orbit. So here we were flying round and round, burning up our last gas, black as pitch outside and nothing but silence on the radio.

Suddenly on our wing was one of our F6Fs! How he found us I don't know. As soon as he peeled off, command called, "Egg crate 3-1-3, you are cleared for a straight approach landing."

They knew we were about out of gas. When we checked the IFF later, *it wasn't working*! We were close to getting taken down by friendly fire.

Another time when got over our target, I noticed our ICS (Inter Communications System) wasn't working. There were several bomb shackles in the bomb bay and several kinds of bombs. The pilot decides what to drop and I set the proper switches. If we were not able to communicate, we were in trouble. After a while, I thought of a way. Our radio transmitter had three main circuits: 1.

modulation, 2. power amplification, 3. Antenna circuit. All three have to be in tune with each other before the transmitter will transmit. Futhermore, these were connected by a coaxual cable for quick repair. What I did was, reach behind my transmitter and unplug my antenna circuit, flip on my radio transmitter, and use it for a back-up ICS. They heard at debriefing what I had done. They instructed every radioman to do the same if their ICS went out.

One day one of our planes returning from a mission missed catching his tail hook on the arresting cable, so he slammed into the barrier cable hard. There were several people on the island and catwalks watching the action. Everybody was real quiet wondering if they were hurt. Then, the radioman popped his head out holding a bleeding finger and hollered, "Purple heart!". With that , everybody let out a roar of laughter.

One of the missions our squadron made was on Osaka and Kobe. It was day time and, by luck, I wasn't on it as I had flown the night before. Several planes flew inland at different places at low altitude, made their pass, and headed back to sea. Osaka and Kobe are back in a bay close together with high ground all around. Their intention was to surprise them but it didn't work. Instead they were caught in a crossfire and got shot up. I don't remember if they all got back, (After all, it was fifty years ago.) I do remember, however, that one TBM with all its tail shot off except one side of its horizontal stabilizer flew over two hundred miles back and landed with no one hurt! The crewmen said all at once his tail just floated away.

Egg crates

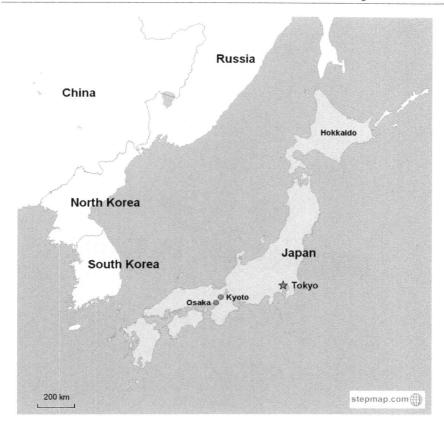

Photo # 80-G-273032   Kamikaze hits USS Essex, 25 November 1944

JAP GRACE SHOT DOWN OFF STARBOARD BOW OF USS WASP (CV 18)
USS BON HOMME RICHARD (CV-31   Notice smoke, smell of gunpowder.

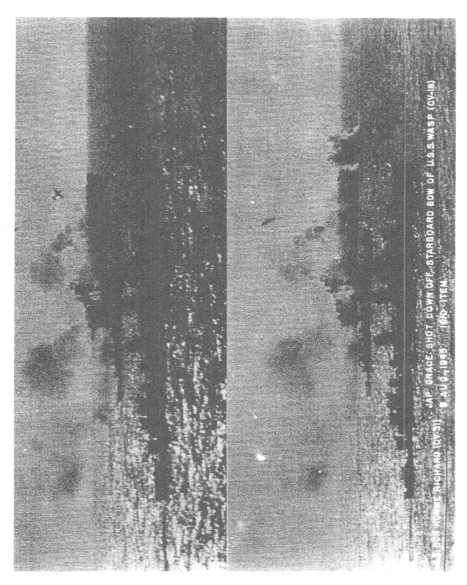

NIGHT FIGHTING SQUADRON 91

Commander Task Group 38.4's Flash Report 131334 of August:

"FLASH REPORT TOMCAT DADCAP X BON HOMME RICHARD BATS UNDER SKILLFUL CONTROL TOMCAT 1 SPLASHED 4 BANDIT GOT 2 PROBABLE KILLS WEST OF FORCE BETWEEN 1835 & 1915 X ALL BUT ONE OF THESE BAGS BY ENSIGN P. T. McDONALD WHO GOT 1 NICK 2 FRANCES AND PROBABLY GOT ANOTHER NICK AND FRANCES X LT. R. T. KIELING ACCOUNTED FOR FOURTH SPLASH WHICH WAS A NICK X"

Commander Task Force 38's despatch 140745 of July:

"ATTENTION ENSIGN MCDONALD X WELL DONE X WE CALEDONIANS ARE PARTICULARLY PROUD OF YOU X MCCAIN X"

Commander Task Force 38's despatch 140753 of July:

"CTG 38.4 131334 X OUR AWARDS BOARD IS WAITING TO HEAR ABOUT MCDONALD X"

ComBatRon 2's despatch 210700 of August:

"THE PLANE SERVICES FURNISHED FOR ALL THREE OF MY BOMBARDMENTS WERE UNIFORMLY EXCELLENT X THE UTMOST COOPERATION WAS EVIDENT DURING PLANNING AND EXECUTION AND I DESIRE TO MAKE KNOWN MY APPRECIATION TO THOSE WHO SO EAGERLY AND CAPABLY CONDUCTED THE AIR OPERATIONS X'

CTG 38.4's summary #4, despatch 182225 of July:

". . . X OUR BATTLESHIPS SCREENED BY DESRON PLUS FRANK
KNOX BOMBARDED TARGETS IN THE HITACHI AREA NORTH OF
TOKYO THE NIGHT BEFORE LAST IN WEATHER THAT PREVENTED
PLANES SPOTTING X PRELIMINARY PHOTO INTERPRETATION
INDICATES THAT THE WHOLE AREA WAS WELL SATURATED AND
THAT THE HITACHI ENGINEERING WORKS AND THE LITCHI ARMS
FACTORY WERE BADLY DAMAGED X THEY WILL PROBABLY BE OUT
OF BUSINESS FOR MANY MONTHS IF NOT FOR THE DURATION X
THE BRITISH BB KING GEORGE JOINED OURS IN THIS INTENSE
BROADSIDE AGAINST THE JAPS X ALL IN ALL IN SPITE OF
MORE THAN OUR SHARE OF INCLEMENT WEATHER I FEEL THAT THE
FIRST PHASE OF OUR OPERATIONS HAS BEEN CARRIED OUT IN A
VERY SATISFACTORY MANNER BY ALL HANDS X I PARTICULARLY COMMEND
AIR GROUP 91 FOR THEIR FINE WORK UNDER DIFFICULT CONDITIONS X"
(TOD 191138)

Commanding Officer, U.S.S. BON HOMME RICHARD's 191220 of July:

"REF MY 191138 IN WHICH CONTAINED CTG 38.4's COMMENDATION
OF CVGN 91 X THE CAPTAIN WISHES TO STATE THAT HE CON-
CURS IN THIS AND ALL PRIOR COMMENDATIONS PLUS ANY MORE
THAT COME IN X" (TOD 191220)

Commander Task Force 38's despatch 262001 of July:

"FOR THE HEADWORK AND TEAMWORK OF THE FIGHTER DIRECTORS
PARTICULARLY IN THE TOMCATS AND WATCHDOG FOR THE PLAN-
NING AND SKILLFUL EXECUTION OF ALL NIGHT STRIKES FOR
THE SUPERBLY COMPETENT NIGHT FIGHTERS AND THEIR DIRECTORS
FOR THE PILOTS WHO PUNCHED THROUGH THE WEATHER TO HIT
THE ISE AND FOR ALL THOSE WHO SMACKED THEIR TARGETS
UNDER TOUGH CONDITIONS CONGRATULATIONS AND WELL DONE X"
MC CAIN X

Commander Task Force 38's despatch 131121 of August:

"ENEMY PLANES SMARTLY HANDLED TODAY X PERFORMANCE OF
CONTROL AND CAP MAGNIFICENT X . . . X INCIDENTALLY
GIVE THE TOMCATS A SAUCER OF CREAM AND THE WATCHDOG
NOT A BONE BUT A STEAK X ACTION SMART THROUGHOUT X
A HEARTY WELL DONE TO ALL HANDS X"

NIGHT FIGHTING SQUADRON 91

"PATS ON THE BACK"

Commander Task Group 38.1 (Rear Admiral J. J. Clark):

"GREATLY APPRECIATE THE FINE WORK YOUR SHIP AND PILOTS HAVE DONE IN PROVIDING DAY PATROLS SINCE JOINING X"
(TOD 081743 June)

Commander Task Force 38, Despatch 151833 of July 1945:

"PUBLISH TO ALL HANDS X DESPITE FOUL WEATHER RESULTS OF THE FORAY HIGHLY CREDITABLE X"

Commander Third Fleet's despatch to Commander Task Force 38:

"HEARTILY CONCUR YOUR 151833 X"

Commander Task Unit 34.8.2's despatch 172045 of July:

"DESIRE EXPRESS APPRECIATION FOR EXCELLENT SERVICE YOUR AIR PICKETS AND VFN X THEIR PARTICIPATION WAS OF UN-ESTIMABLE VALUE THIS GROUP X AIR PICKETS DID AN OUT-STANDING JOB X PLEASE PASS ABOVE TO PILOTS CONCERNED X I TRUST ALL PILOTS RETURNED SAFELY X"
Rear Admiral O. C. Badger.

Commander Task Group 38.4 (Rear Admiral A. W. Radford):

"I AM SURE YOU GAVE THE NIPS A BAD NIGHT X IT WAS A TOUGH JOB VERY WELL DONE X AM VERY GLAD AIRCRAFT DID SO WELL UNDER SUCH DIFFICULT CIRCUMSTANCES X HOPE WE CAN GET TOGETHER SOON WITH INFO ADDRESSEES TO DISCUSS FUTURE OPERATIONS OF THIS KIND X"

Commander Carrier Division 7's despatch 180732 of July:

"WELL DONE TO ALL CONCERNED WITH RECOVERING AIRCRAFT LAST NIGHT X PLEASE EXPRESS TO CAG 91 AND THE PILOTS CONCERNED MY ADMIRATION FOR THE SUPERB AIRMANSHIP DIS-PLAYED UNDER FLYING CONDITIONS WHICH WOULD HAVE BEEN CONSIDERED EXTREMELY DANGEROUS IN DAYLIGHT X OPERATION INDICATES A HIGH DEGREE OF TRAINING SKILL AND MORALE IN THE AIR GROUP X"
Rear Admiral J. J. Ballentine

We went into Leyte Gulf in the Philippine Islands for some R&R (Rest and Relaxation). We were anchored with several other ships. The Navy threw a big beer party on the beach. They had beer and soft drinks and things to eat for a large crowd. I was walking the beach with a friend when I looked up and saw a boy coming toward me who I had graduated with me from high school. He was 'Box Head' Stone. Later a Filipino came up to us trying to sell us some homemade Japanese liquor in a catsup bottle. We laughed, and my friend said, "Let's see you drink it." The Philippino couldn't get the top off fast enough to take a drink. His face got red, his eyes ran tears, and he couldn't stop coughing. We said, "That's what we thought."

As I was getting on the landing craft to take us back to the ship, another Philippino came up to me and pinched my skivvy shirt and pointed to a big pineapple. He wanted to trade. I peeled off my shirt and gave it to him. I took the pineapple back to the ship.

Before each mission we were briefed and after debriefed. Day squadrons had pictures from their gun camera to show. We had none, so Rip unofficially rigged up a flare in our bomb bay with a release wire going to the cockpit. All our regular bomb shackles were being used. So, one night when we got through bombing an air field, we flew about five hundred feet over it and Rip pulled the release wire. I didn't even know he had a flare. I started screaming in the mike, "It's still in there!" We were now a bright lit up target for all the guns below. We bounced and bounced until it finally fell free. Forget the pictures! Get out of here! As soon as we got back to the ship, Rip put his arm around my shoulders and said, "Don't you tell." I didn't.

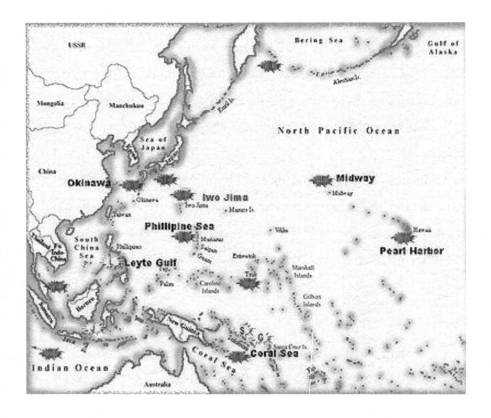

Chapter 14 *After the battles*

When the United States dropped the atomic bomb, we were glad. Nobody felt sorry for the Japanese people. We were just glad it was going to end and we wouldn't have to send troops into Japan. In hind sight, it probably saved my life and a lot of American and Japanese people as well. I used to utter a little prayer, just as we rolled over into a dive. "God have mercy on me and the people below."

After the atomic bomb was dropped, there were two or three weeks of cease fire before the surrender papers were signed. Saying you have cease fire and having one are two different things. We had some planes from the York Town aircraft carrier shot down after the cease fire. As a result, Admiral Halsey ordered all Japanese planes to be shot down, but in a *friendly manner*.

Soon after the cease fire, we flew over Japan looking things over. I remember making a pass over a Japanese airfield. We descended at about a thirty-degree angle picking up a lot of speed. We went by the tower at eye level and about as close as we could get without hitting it. I still remember looking eye ball to eye ball with the man in the tower. They didn't shoot.

After they stopped shooting at us, we searched every day for about two weeks for POW camps. When we found them, we would come in just above the fence and drop canvas bags full of food and candy rolled up in skivvy shirts. Looking out my window was a row of brown skinny guys, with their bones showing, grinning back at me. Without asking anyone, I stole most all of the magazines from the ship's library. I rolled them up in a tight roll and tied them good with string. When we dropped the food, I shoved out some magazines.

We had to search long and wide to find the camps. They were usually in mountainous regions. We had to fly low enough to determine if the people were American or Asian or Japanese. The mountains were very steep, and many were terraced.

Photo # 80-G-490386   Allied Prisoners of War wave at Navy plane, 25 Aug. 1945

One day we were down in a narrow valley with steep mountains on each side about one thousand feet in the air. As we came around a bend, Rip threw the plane into a severe climb. We were in a box end canyon and the only way out was to climb over. The pitch of the engine changed as it strained. The plane began to vibrate, and the stall horn was blasting. As we continued to slow and shake, I said to myself, "Well, this is it."

Finally, we got over, barely missing the rocks. I could see every detail of those rocks. As soon as we were over, we had to glide down the other side to pick up speed.

On our way back to the ship, we flew over Tokyo to see the umbrellas. The streets were full of people with bright colored umbrellas. As we went over at five hundred feet altitude we could see all those umbrellas up turn to look up at us. We had done this on other trips and thought it was funny.

When we were flying missions looking for prisoners of war camps and there was no shooting, a boy in the ship's crew from Nashville, like me, wanted to go and see Japan. None of the ship's crew had ever seen Japan. I got permission to let him go up in the empty turret. He was a big mama's boy, over six feet tall. I got him down by the lockers and adjusted a parachute to fit him. It was a nice sunny day and when the time came for us to climb aboard, he stalled and refused to get in. There were a lot of people on the island watching us. As I looked at the crowd of faces, I spotted a boy I knew from Memphis. I hollered, "Clement! Get down here!" He ran all the way down to the plane. We switched the parachute harness from the first guy to Clement, even though it didn't fit, and we took off. He sure got an eye full. Afterwards, he thanked me every time I saw him. He had something to tell when he got home.

On the POW missions, we usually flew in pairs of one TBM and one F6F. On our way to and from Japan, the F6F would fly on our wing. One day about twenty minutes after we left Japan the fighter pilot radioed that he had an oil problem and didn't think he could make it back to the ship. We turned and went back to Japan with him.

Just off the mainland was an island with a big, green flat field. We came in right on his wing when he landed. He rolled a short distance and stood up on his nose. We made a tight turn and came around to land with our wheels and flaps down, intending to land a short distance away. By this time, the fighter plane pilot had managed to jump out and was running out in front of us giving us the wave off signal. We had to go off and leave him. He got back to the ship a few weeks later with some audacious stories.

80-G-455740 Prisoner of War Camp # 183, at Kobe, Japan

Title: Prisoner of War Camp # 183, at Kobe, Japan
Description: Photographed from a USS Bon Homme Richard (CV-31) aircraft, 6 September 1945. Note U.S. flag flying from the camp's main building and burned out structures across the street from the camp. Official U.S. Navy Photograph, now in the collections of the National Archives.
Catalog #: 80-G-455740
Related Content
Document Type

When I first got on the ship, I was issued a S & W 38 Special with a shoulder holster.

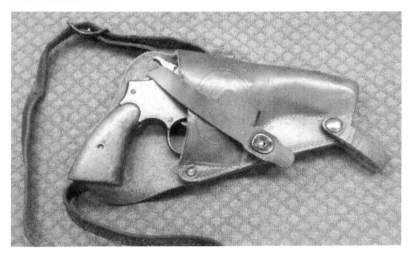

I had worn it for several months but had never fired it. They would not let us shoot it on the ship. So, one day coming back to the ship, I climbed in the empty turret, opened a window hatch and began to fire at the white caps on the ocean. Just as I had my pistol raised to fire, our fighter escort joined up from underneath into the slot where I was shooting. Our startled eyes met, he saw the pistol and was gone in a flash.

Chapter 15 *Signing of surrender*

When the Japanese signed the surrender papers on the battle ship, Missouri, there were B29s flying high overhead and down at 500 feet were Navy planes. I think, by luck, we were right in the center. So, I got to fly almost right over the top. I could see a lot of details.

A short time after this, our ship led several other ships into Tokyo Bay. On our port side were the docks of Yokohama and others. They had some large ships. As we glided by in the calm water of the bay, we looked the Japanese sailors square in the eye. We dropped anchor and stayed there for about two weeks. (about 9-22-45) We went ashore in groups and carried 'K' rations to eat.

There were a few buildings left standing. Sewer lines were burst. We later went to Hiroshima where the first atomic bomb was dropped. Hollow buildings, lone smoke stacks and burnt metal roofing was what we saw. I walked several blocks. I came upon a large pile of ceramic salt and pepper shakers what had survived the blast. I decided I would take some home as a souvenir and picked up some. Then I saw some Japanese were watching me closely with a frown on their faces, so I decided to throw them down. It's a good thing I did because they may have been radioactive.

I saw several Japanese making a fuss over a black ball about two and one-half inches in diameter. It thought it was a rubber ball until one of them took a knife and sliced into it. It was bright orange inside showing it to be a piece of cheese from a 'K' ration box. Coal soot was everywhere, so when they handled the cheese, it became black. They were not accustomed to cheese.

In Yokohoma, several of us were walking the streets just looking around. We crossed a small bridge over a canal and noticed on the other side was a small ticket house with a Japanese woman or girl. We she saw us coming, she took off running. The Japanese leaders had told their people that Americans would kill and rape. *(By the way that is what the Japanese did in China, the Philippines, and all Asia. In the rape of Nanking, the Japanese killed more people than the bomb did in Hiroshima. It is estimated they killed 350,000 or higher.)* We were probably the first Americans she had seen. We were about to go back to our ship and I had an extra 'K' ration box. I left it in her ticket window.

Chapter 15 On our way home

We left Tokyo Bay and made out way to Guam where we dropped anchor in the middle of the bay. The we moved most of our planes onto the flight deck and tied them down. Cots were set up in the hanger deck. Soon we had the whole hanger deck full of marines going home.

We had so many soldiers on board the hall ran twenty-four hours a day. My time to eat may have been at any odd hour.

After eighteen days a sea, we arrived at San Francisco on October 19, 1945. We were the leader in the home coming parade. Behind us was the carrier, York Town, followed by the light cruiser, Oakland, and the destroyer, Buchanan. There were many people on the Golden Gate Bridge cheering as we went under. Horns, tug boat whistles, fire boat spraying water into the air, and boat loads of people cheering welcomed us into port.

It was good to be home! Anywhere in the USA was home!

The enlisted men of the squadron had a dinner banquet in the ball room of the St. Francis Hotel. While on board ship we were paid only ten dollars per month, we did not need much except at the ship's stores. Cigarettes cost $.50 per carton. All our squadron were going home on leave, so they gave us our full back pay. I bought travels checks to take home.

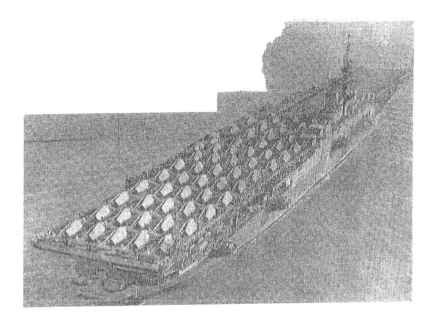

CV-31   BON HOMME R

Wings folded.

Leader of Home-Coming Parade

Under clear skies, a second force of Third Fleet ships came back from the war yesterday, steaming through the Golden Gate to the accompaniment of tugboat whistles, roaring planes and cheers of welcome from crowds on the Gate bridge. The naval parade was led by the aircraft carrier Bon Homme Richard (below), with her air-craft lined up aft, wings folded. On her flight deck, her crew stood smartly in formation. Behind her came the flattop York-town, the light cruiser Oakland and the destroyer Buchanan. Together they brought 3728 discharge-bound fighting men besides their liberty-hungry crews. (Story and pictures of the homecoming on Page 5.)

CV-31

After Radioman-Radar training at Middleton, Tennessee.

Photo # NH 97341   USS Bon Homme Richard off New York City, January 1945

ALL STATIONS V AIR PLOT,.MESSG FROM CTF 38 X LATEST SUMMARY

COMPLETE,.EXCEPT FOR LAST STRIKE X ONLY 13 BANDITS,.IN

AIR OVER LAND X ALL AVOIDED COMBAT X TWO,.TWIN SNOOPERS

SPLASHED NEAR TASK FORCE X,.95 PLANES ON MANY FIELDS

DESTROYED AND 137,.DAMAGED X OUR LOSSES 3 CORSAIRS

AND 5 AVEN,.GERS TO AA X HIS 101033X,.NOW UNDER RADIO SILENCE

L.E.AGEE ARM2c

Wings Folded

Into Japan

Peace at Last

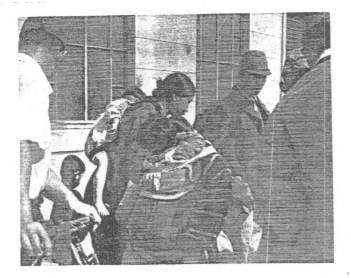

Paintings
by Lucius Agee

f

Lucius Agee wearing his flight jacket.

v

Fourteen buttons

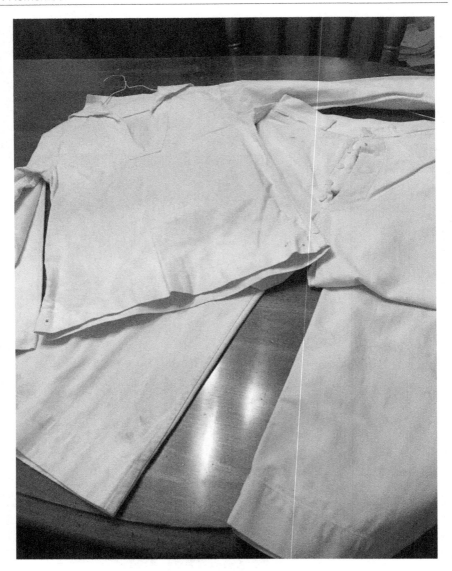

Made in the USA
Columbia, SC
21 April 2018